This book belongs to

_____

_____

NORTH STAR BOOKS

The

Fishing Fleets

of

New England

The Fishing Fleets

HOUGHTON MIFFLIN COMPANY BOSTON

NORTH STAR BOOKS

of New England

MARY ELLEN CHASE

Illustrated with photographs and prints

THE RIVERSIDE PRESS CAMBRIDGE   1961

THANKS are due to the Gloucester Chamber of Commerce; the *Gloucester Daily Times;* The Peabody Museum of Salem; the United States Fish and Wildlife Service; the Mariners Museum, Newport News; Gorton's of Gloucester, Inc.; United Press International; Yale University Art Gallery; the William L. Clements Library, University of Michigan; Mr. William A. Baker; and Mr. Storer B. Lunt and W. W. Norton & Company, Inc., for the use of the illustrations in this volume. The illustration on the title page is from the collection of the Peabody Museum.

Special thanks are also due to Captain Morton Selig of Gloucester who checked the manuscript.

Books by

MARY ELLEN CHASE

A Goodly Heritage

Mary Peters

Silas Crockett

Dawn in Lyonesse

Jonathan Fisher: Maine Parson

Windswept

The Bible and the Common Reader

The Plum Tree

The White Gate

Life and Language in the Old Testament

The Edge of Darkness

The Lovely Ambition

Sailing the Seven Seas

Donald McKay and the Clipper Ships

The Fishing Fleets of New England

Photographic Credits

CONTENTS

Several historians believe that before Columbus "discovered" America—possibly many years preceding that great event—fishermen from the ports of Europe were crossing the North Atlantic in search of cod.

Catholic countries needed fish in great quantities, particularly during the season of Lent. And so, despite fear of fiends, demons and sea monsters; despite fog, icebergs and storms, little sailing ships, with many a prayer for safety, set forth on their westward voyage to drop their baited lines over the Grand Banks where cod in countless millions were waiting to take the hook.

Francis Parkman says that in 1517 (more than a century before the first voyage of the Mayflower*) "fifty Castilian, French and Portuguese vessels" were engaged in fishing these coastal waters. And there has probably been no year since in which a gleaming harvest has not been reaped from beneath these fog-enshrouded seas.*

Mary Ellen Chase, a daughter of Maine and a life-long student of seafaring, has written an intriguing history of codfishing over the past three hundred and fifty years. Here are the men who risked their lives scores of times during each fishing season to bring home their salted cargo—the intrepid fishermen who took their little schooners into the teeth of many a northeast gale, and all too often failed to return to the New England village where wife and children awaited them.

Those who have read Captains Courageous *by Rudyard Kipling need no additional introduction to this volume. And for these, and all others who love sea adventure, here is another fascinating book dedicated to the courage and independence which has marked all fishermen of the New England Coast. Those who "go down to the sea in ships" will always have our envy and our admiration.*

STERLING NORTH
General Editor

FOREWORD

THERE ARE, of course, many kinds of fish in the
waters off our coasts, many ways of catching them,
and countless boats which for over three centuries
of our history have set out from many harbors
bound for those areas of the sea where fish are
most numerous. There have been many thousands
of men and boys who have followed this dangerous
calling, some going out after shellfish—lobsters or
scallops or oysters—others after tuna or halibut,
mackerel or the elusive herring, still others after
mammoth whales in every ocean.

The cod, however, has always been the basis of
New England fishing. In this book I shall tell the
story of the skippers and crews of New England
who, over a period of three hundred years and
more, have risked their lives, and not infrequently
lost them, in its pursuit.

For the cod, not only the most plentiful fish,
but the humblest in terms of food, has had a great
deal to do with the history of New England, which
means to a large extent the history of our country
as a whole. It early became, in fact, such a well-
recognized symbol of that history that in March,
1784, a wooden codfish was, upon the action of
the General Court of Massachusetts, hung opposite
the Speaker's desk in the Massachusetts Hall of
Representatives of the Old State House in Boston.
It is still there beneath the golden dome of the

present State Capitol on Beacon Hill.

Yet behind the codfishing fleets of New England rise the dim shapes of many other small ships which, a century and more before the Pilgrims came to Plymouth, ventured forth from French harbors, from English, Portuguese, and Spanish seaports, to cross the perilous, unknown Atlantic toward Newfoundland, Labrador, the Gulf of Maine, after the cod swimming in countless millions in those cold waters. The story of these earlier brave mariners must not be forgotten in any book about our own adventures in fishing. Let us, then, dedicate our first pages to them and turn our thoughts and our imaginations backward some four or five hundred years to foreign men and boys, long since dead, who, with incredible courage, began the history of codfishing off our forbidding North American shores.

Mary Ellen Chase

Northampton, Massachusetts
July, 1960

This book is dedicated to my nieces,

Edith Lord Chase

and

Margaret Spencer Chase

1

The First Fishermen from Europe

SOME DAYS AGO, while I was telling a well-known American maritime historian about this book on our fishing fleets, he said with the enthusiasm of a boy, though he is no longer young:

"Don't forget to tell them about *Captains Courageous*. What a kick I got out of that book when I was a kid! And I've read it a dozen times since. There's just nothing like it to give the real truth about fishing off the Banks."

He is quite right. I, too, remember the thrill I got when I was twelve or thirteen from Rudyard Kipling's wonderful story; and I have

just reread it to see if the years have lessened
its power and charm. They haven't, in the least.
So — if any reader now beginning these pages
does not know about Harvey Cheyne, the
spoiled son of a multimillionaire, his fall from
the deck of a luxurious liner making her way
toward Europe, his rescue by Manuel, the
Portuguese sailor, in the rocking dory of the
fishing schooner *We're Here,* and his conver-
sion through months of difficult and dangerous

Crew members of a Fisherman

shing schooner *Elsie* under the command of Capt. Morton Selig

toil from an obnoxious and worthless nuisance to a decent and promising young man — such a reader would best procure *Captains Courageous* from the nearest public library and read it before continuing with this book. It will be an admirable preface to my own.

Harvey learned a great deal, and often in the hard way, from Disko Troop, the stern yet just skipper of the *We're Here,* from Dan, the skipper's son, and from all the wet, weary fishermen on that Gloucester schooner where he worked as he had never worked before. What he apparently did not learn was that centuries before his time other boys with strange tongues had stretched out their aching bones on bunks far more uncomfortable even than his, had been tossed relentlessly about on heavy, gray seas, and had like him longed for dry clothing and soft beds. Perhaps Kipling himself, who was a novelist rather than a historian,

did not know about those early fishermen. Yet no story of our own fleets is complete without them; and to them we shall now turn.

Tradition, though no actual historical record, claims that there were fishing boats from Western Europe off the coasts of Labrador and Newfoundland long before John Cabot made his first voyage to America in 1497. In a description which Cabot gave of his voyage he tells of the vast number of fish in these northern waters. "The sea is covered with fishes," he says, "which are caught not only with the net but in baskets, a stone being tied to them in order that the baskets may sink in the water." He says, too, that the "Savages" call the cod *baccalaos,* a Basque word used by sailors from the Bay of Biscay off northern Spain. Modern scholars question the strictly Basque origin of this word, although they do grant that it is a corruption of several similar names for cod used in the Spanish and Portuguese tongues and dialects. So fine a historian as Francis Parkman, in his *Pioneers of France in the New World,* feels certain that the use of this word alone among the Newfoundland natives proves the presence of fishermen from the Iberian peninsula there as early as the mid-fifteenth century. And he may well be right.

The first authentic and dependable record of this fishing, however, is of the year 1504, when some small, sturdy vessels from Brittany, in northern France, probably from the port of St. Malo, that old town of gray walls and many ships, set forth for the waters off Newfoundland and left the name of Cape Breton Island as an enduring trace of their early voyages. In 1510, it is said, fish taken from the waters of the "New Land" were for sale in the market place of Rouen. In 1517 there were 50 fishing boats off Newfoundland; sixty years later, in 1577, there were 315, from France 150, from Spain 100, from Portugal 50, and from England only 15.

Sixteenth-century sailing ship

English fishermen, since the early fifteenth century, favored the northern seas off Iceland for their catch and were later than those from countries farther south to drop their lines and nets in North American waters. They received encouragement, however, from various Acts of Parliament enacted in 1548 and succeeding years, for these Acts imposed heavy fines on persons who should eat meat on the fast days prescribed by the Church; and long before the sixteenth century had passed, English fishing craft from Southampton, Plymouth, Falmouth, and a score of smaller ports were joining those of St. Malo, Dieppe, Bilboa, and Lisbon. In 1594 Plymouth alone had boats "estimated at 100."

As every student of early American history knows, during the hundred years between the voyages of Jacques Cartier in 1534 until the permanent settlement of Massachusetts, explorers as well as fishermen were braving the seas off the Gulf of St. Lawrence and along New England shores. These men were largely from France and England. Most of these hardy adventurers mention the abundance of fish.

Cartier found French fishing vessels in the Straits of Belle Isle between Newfoundland and Labrador, and rude settlements of fishermen on Newfoundland. Samuel de Champlain found both, too, when in 1603 he made a voyage to the St. Lawrence and in 1604 sailed along the Maine coast, naming certain of its islands and headlands, and continuing to Massachusetts Bay.

The Englishman Bartholomew Gosnold in 1602 named Cape Cod after its "multitudes" of fish and even declared that the fishing there was superior to that off Newfoundland. Indeed, he says that the cod were so abundant that they "did vex" his ship. Martin Pring, coming from Bristol, England, in 1603, agreed with Gosnold; and George Waymouth two

years later felt equally sure that the fish off the Maine coast were "much greater and better fed" than those in the more stormy, far colder northern seas.

The explorers, of course, were not after codfish. They were sent out by rich merchants, or by other men of rank and position who were adventurers at heart, or even by the kings of France and England. They called themselves "gentlemen" and surely felt far removed from the crude fishermen who followed the sea only to provide a means of livelihood for their families.

Explorers were bent upon the annexation of new lands for their French and English sovereigns. They wanted to discover mines of gold and silver and copper, being anxious to obtain for their own countries wealth equal to that rumored of Spanish *conquistadores* in the Southwest, in Peru, Mexico, and California. They had dreams of a Northwest Passage to Asia and the fabled wealth of "the Indies." They had dreams, too, of fame and fortune,

A stretch of coast near Cutler, Maine

titles and lands, when once they should sail
their high-prowed, square-sailed ships back
home to receive homage and glory for their
daring exploits.

They had, it is true, thoughts of colonies on
the rocky, rugged shores and islands and, with
the backing of their patrons at home, made
attempts to establish such outposts along the
St. Lawrence River, in Newfoundland, Nova
Scotia, and on the coast of Maine — rude set-

tlements which should serve as bases for the fishermen and for the fur traders who followed them. The French, with their genius for dealing with the Indians and their early zeal for missionary labor among them, had far better success with their first colonies in New France than did the English, who failed until the days of the Pilgrims and the Puritans to give permanence to any of their tiny settlements along New England shores.

When one looks back upon those faraway voyages to North American waters and tries to visualize what must have happened during the sixteenth and early seventeenth centuries in those many tossing ships, it seems a pity that so little is known about the fishermen who made up their adventuresome crews. It is said that one Frenchman, named Scavelet, made forty voyages to Newfoundland after codfish before the year 1609. If he did, he clearly did not think his courage and discomfort worth recording, even though, which is improbable, he had been able to write. Information about

Early fishing station in Newfoundland.
Cod are drying in the foreground.

These are reconstructions of the ships that brought
the colonists to Jamestown in 1607.

the explorers is scarce enough; nothing what-
soever remains about the daring and the peril
of the thousands of fishermen drawing up the
teeming riches of the seas. Their tiny vessels
are phantoms, and they themselves are but
ghosts.

Yet upon the fish which they caught, salted,
and stowed away in their holds depends much

They are similar to the types of vessels that were used for fishing during this period.

of the early history of our country. Plymouth and Massachusetts Bay would hardly have promised new homes to our forefathers, high-minded though they were, had they not known that the sea had already provided food and hard-earned wages for thousands of nameless and undistinguished men long before their day.

They did not come, as we so often think, to

a completely uncharted wilderness, to a wholly unknown land. Capes, harbors, and islands had been explored; New England, thanks to Captain John Smith, had been quite fully described and even named. In his fascinating "Description" of it, published in England in 1616, he "speaks much of fishing." Fish, he says, are "a mean and a base commodity" and may seem "a contemptible trade," and yet it will become a source of greater treasure than the gold and silver mines of the King of Spain.

In such sayings Captain Smith proved himself to be no mean prophet. Before the coming of the Pilgrims in 1620 fish had opened up trade with foreign countries, from the islands of the West Indies to the ports of France. Perhaps it is not too much to say that the glory of our American merchant ships in the nineteenth century which spread their great sails toward the Far East had its lowly beginning in the inglorious codfish, which four, and possibly five, centuries prior to their day had lured countless strangers to seek our stormy coasts.

2

Early New England Fishermen

THE BUSY FISHERIES on Monhegan and in the Pemaquid region of Maine are among the earliest of which we have record. Captain John Smith, if he did not, indeed, originate them, was surely for several years the ruling spirit among them. He was there with two ships in the spring of 1614; in 1615 there were six fishing vessels under his charge, and in 1616, eight; and, although he does not specify the exact location of those in the two later years, it is not unlikely that they fished in or near the same waters, especially in view of a visit from a member of the Plymouth colony some few years later in the spring of 1622.

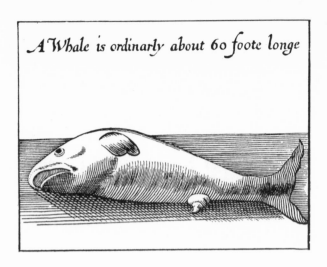

A Whale is ordinarly about 60 foote longe

Captain Smith says in his enticing *Description of New England* that his first "plot" or plan in 1614 was "to take whales" and to search for mines of gold and copper. The whales, though there were many, proved not to be those yielding oil; there was no gold or copper; but there were codfish, he writes, in far greater number than off Newfoundland.

When the whale comes aboue water y̌ ſhallop rowes towards him and being within reach of him the harpoiner darts his harpingiron at him out of both his hands and being faſt they lance him to death

In this year of 1614 he and his men dried 40,000 cod by placing them on "flakes," which were woven platforms made of alder or birch branches and erected on posts some three feet above the ground and upon which the split

The whale is cut up as hee lyes floting crofse the ftearne of a fhipp the blubber is cut from the flefh by peeces 3 or 4 foote long and being rafed is rowed on fhore towards the coppers

fish would get the sun and the wind. These dried fish Smith sent to Spain in one of his ships. In the other he carried 7000 "cor" or salted fish, that is, pickled in brine, back to England together with "near 1100 beaver skins, 100 martens, and near as many otters" which

These are seventeenth-century illustrations of whaling.

They place 2.or 3.coppers on a roe and ẙ chopping boat on the one side and the cooling boate on the other side to receiue ẙ oyle of ẙ coppers, the chopt blubber being boyled is taken out of the coppers and put in wiker baskets or barowes throwg wch the oyle is dreaned and runes into ẙ cooler wch is ½ fall of water out of wch it is convaied by troughs into buts or hogsheads

he had got from the Indians in return for what he calls "trifles."

When he was not fishing, this redoubtable captain "ranged the coast both east and west" in a small boat to see what manner of country this New England was. It apparently delighted him, its "high craggy, cliffy rocks," its "divers sandy bays," its lands "fit for pasture," its great variety of trees, and particularly its excellent harbors. "Of all the four parts of the world that I have seen," he writes, "I would rather live here than anywhere."

It has long seemed to me, and to many others as well, that Americans have not given Captain John Smith the recognition he deserves as one of our earliest pioneers, map makers, explorers, and, above all else in its long effects, fishermen. We are far too given to connecting him only with the 1607 Virginian colony at Jamestown, where his hotheaded, perhaps overbearing nature brought him into frequent conflict, even though there, too, his was the ruling spirit. He was a man of tremendous physical and moral endurance, of almost incredible courage and optimism, and one also of vaulting ambition for the future of his

Captain John Smith at the age of thirty-seven

country and his countrymen. He could not bear even the thought that France or Spain should outdo England in the work of colonization or in the amassing of wealth, whether that wealth should lie in gold and silver, or in furs and fish.

His writings, which he humbly calls "rude," are among the most enlivening of reading. He apparently felt more contempt and scorn for an idle man than even for a knave or a fool, and again and again he urges upon Englishmen the settlement of New England so that men through a rugged life in a new land may be shaken out of their inertia and laziness.

The famous saying, attributed to him in Virginia, "He who will not work shall not eat," is echoed in his *Description of New England* when he says that even young boys and girls, unless they are "very idle," can surely carry fish to the flakes and turn them over there, and that no woman is so old that she cannot spin threads for nets to catch them. "In the harbors," he writes, "a little boy might take of

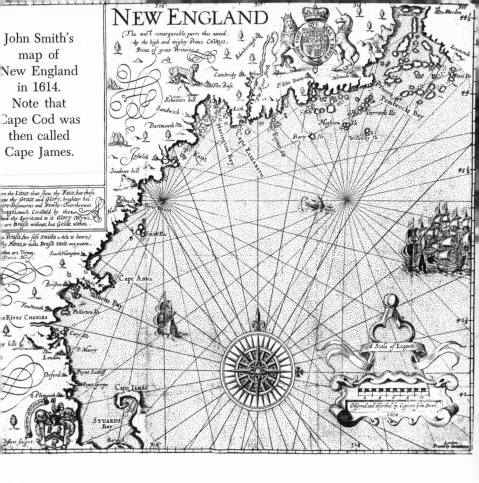

cunners and such delicate fish, at the ship's
stern more than six or ten can eat in a day."
He writes, too, of the fun in fishing as well as
its actual gain in money. "Before their own
doors in their own boats upon the sea," a man,
woman, or child "with a small hook and line"
may pull up at this "pretty sport" twopence,

or sixpence, or twelvepence, "two or three hundred cods" in one day. John Smith was one of our most ardent fishermen three hundred and fifty years ago, and no story of American fishing could be complete without him!

As for the Pilgrims, there is, indeed, little evidence that they ever seriously took to fishing. They had, as we remember, originally intended to settle a hundred miles farther to the south, very likely in the region of Manhattan Island; and only bad weather drove them to Cape Cod. Unlike the Puritans under Winthrop's charge, they had brought with them no apparatus for fishing, neither boats nor supplies such as nets, tackle, and salt for drying, and no dedicated fishermen.

One of their number, Edward Winslow, writes in 1621 that they have "fish and fowl" in abundance, that there are lobsters, eels, and mussels in plenty. The "divers shell fish" could be, as he says, "taken with the hands," and the bays and brooks were filled with bass and other fish. Yet he writes, too, of their lack of

Reconstruction of a typical
seventeenth-century fishing vessel

fishing gear which prohibits them from any offshore fishing. They must have been in severe straits for food in the spring of their second year at Plymouth, for, having heard of thirty English vessels engaged in fishing off Monhegan Island, they sent Winslow there to beg provisions for their hunger.

But although the Pilgrims at Plymouth did not launch their boats far out into the deep

after cod, either because of lack of proper fishing gear or perhaps of desire, there were men shortly following them who did. By the year 1623 there were not only numerous fishermen from England off the coast of Maine, but others on the waters near Cape Ann, who made also an attempt to weather the winter of 1623–24 on that forbidding coast. About the same year fishing stations for the drying and curing of cod were established at the mouth of the Piscataqua River and of the Merrimac, on the

Isles of Shoals, which some forty years later could boast of fifteen hundred fishermen, and before 1630 in Marblehead, Gloucester, and Salem. Many of these early ventures were doomed to failure so far as the sparse records of them give any dependable evidence; but they prove at least a continuous interest in fishing and the realization that it was the industry upon which New England must depend for survival during her first years.

One of the earliest and surely one of the

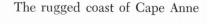

The rugged coast of Cape Anne

most excited among New England fishermen was John Winthrop, Governor of the Massachusetts Bay Colony. On his voyage here in 1630 he enters in his Journal for June 7th the astounding fact that from the waters, probably near Mount Desert Island as they sailed southward, the men on his ship in less than two hours and with only a few hooks caught sixty-seven codfish! "Most of them very great fish," he writes, "some a yard and a half long." He

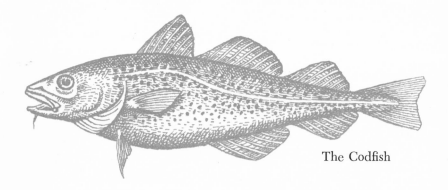

The Codfish

goes on to say how very good they tasted, since the salt fish which his ship, the *Arbella,* and the two others accompanying her had carried for their long journey was entirely "spent."

By the time the surprised Governor Winthrop dropped his line over the side of the *Arbella* and three days later landed to take over the destinies of the Massachusetts Bay Colony, he found another sort of line of lonely, busy, widely scattered fishing stations along the rocky coasts of his new home, from Cape Cod and Cape Ann north to Monhegan and Pemaquid and the mouth of the Kennebec in the province of Maine.

The life on these early fishing stations must have been a lonely and perilous one which demanded adventuresome and sturdy souls. When the stations were established in the first

decades of the seventeenth century, the fishermen from various English seaports stayed only
long enough to catch and to cure their fish.
Then they sailed away with their cargoes.
Their residence on the headlands and rocky
islands of New England was, like the fish flakes
they erected, but temporary, to be borne but
for a brief season. As early as 1635, however,
English merchants began to encourage, for
reasons of economy, the maintenance of such
stations throughout the entire year, the building of homes, even the bringing over of
families.

We know at least something about one of
these isolated fishing colonies through the
letters of a certain John Winter, who wrote
frequently to his employer, Robert Trelawney,
a merchant in Plymouth, England. John Winter's station, the largest and perhaps the most
important of all these early New England fishing communities, was located on Richmond's
Island, a small island off Cape Elizabeth near
what is now Portland, Maine.

Winter was the superintendent, or agent, in charge of this outpost, and without doubt he whiled away the long evenings and the northeast gales of a Maine winter by writing his reports. Through these we know that his wife summoned up the courage to come over with him to cook for his fishermen and that his daughter Sarah came also. Apparently two clergymen, the first named Richard Gibson and a later one named Robert Jordan, braved the stormy Atlantic to minister to the spiritual needs of the fishermen and perhaps to provide companionship for Sarah's long days.

John Winter quite clearly had his troubles in this unusual life so far from home and from any of the amenities of civilization. Without doubt Mrs. Winter had hers, too! Certain of the servants, he writes, are "slothful enough." The best of them all on one tragic day is caught by the tide and drowned. Bears on the nearby mainland are a menace both by carrying away the pigs, evidently brought from England, and by stealing the drying fish at night. Rival fishermen from Massachusetts stations break down the flakes. There are rumors of pirates, under the ferocious "Dixie Bull," making depredations in the Pemaquid region. Indians are a constant danger.

Nevertheless, Winter keeps his boats at sea the year round, sometimes employing as many as sixty fishermen, and continues to ship dried fish to all manner of European ports. In his odd hours he tends "a kitchen garden" on his island and raises many kinds of home vegetables. He lived six years on Richmond's, from 1639 until 1645, the year of his death; and he has contributed more than a little to the early history of New England fishing simply by telling us something of the life on remote stations like his own.

By the middle of the seventeenth century, or at least by the year 1660, the fishing industry of New England had expanded to almost unbelievable size and importance. In place of remote and temporary fishing stations, manned in the northern wilderness by Englishmen like

Cod were still dried on racks in Gloucester
in the early years of this century.

Captain John Smith on Monhegan and John Winter on Richmond's Island, native New Englanders were going forth in their home-made boats from scores of thriving fishing settlements on Cape Ann and Cape Cod, at the mouths of the Merrimac and the Piscataqua rivers, on the Isles of Shoals, and on the frontier coast and islands of the Massachusetts province of Maine, at Pemaquid and Cape Porpoise, on the Damariscove Islands and Matinicus, in Falmouth, and as far eastward as Penobscot Bay. In the year 1664 Boston, then a town of some 14,000 people, had, according to a writer of that day, a fishing fleet of 1300 boats; and it was in the same year that the Isles of Shoals boasted its 1500 fishermen.

In this seventeenth century the most important fishing community of New England was Marblehead. As early as the year 1633 a thriving fishing station was established there; and in the years which followed fisherfolk from Cornwall and the Channel Islands were attracted to its rocky peninsula and its ample harbor as a permanent place for settlement. These fishermen of Marblehead were a vigorous and exclusive lot whose forebears had followed the sea for centuries; and their bold headland sheltered a harbor more prosperous and famous as a fishing port than Gloucester, which did not defeat Marblehead in this respect until the early nineteenth century.

The men and the women of Marblehead were bold, too. They feared, it is said, neither God nor the Devil any more than they feared the monstrous rollers which crashed upon their shores. Their fishing fleets until the War of the Revolution possessed the stoutest and most seaworthy boats in all New England. These Marbleheaders did not share the religious convictions of the Pilgrims and the Puritans. Their ancestors, they said scornfully, did not come to New England for religious freedom, but to catch fish. And catch fish they did, from generation to generation, at the same time building up a foreign trade of their own which made even Salem across the bay envious.

The importance of fishing to the life of colonial New England was recognized early by the General Court of Massachusetts, which by 1635 was enacting laws both for its protection and its encouragement. In that year the Court appointed a commission of six men for the overseeing and management of the "fish trade." Four years later it exempted fishing vessels from public taxes for seven years and all fishermen, as well as ship carpenters, from local military training. Other following laws ensured free land for the erection of fish flakes and free meadow acreage for those fishermen who kept cattle and farmed as most of them did between their voyages. The Court went so far in its concern for fish and fishing that it forbade the use of cod as a fertilizer of barren soil, a practice which the Massachusetts colonists had learned from the Indians. Fish of lesser importance than the cod should be used for manure!

A late seventeenth-century vessel

It was not until the year 1670 that the fishermen of New England set their square sails for the Grand Banks of Newfoundland. There had been, it is true, a few earlier voyages to Nova Scotia under the patronage of ambitious Boston merchants and at least one to the Bay of Islands in Newfoundland, though none of these was notably successful. For the most part, however, during the first half century of the colonial period Massachusetts,

Maine, and New Hampshire fishermen stayed on their own fishing grounds, which meant primarily those off the Maine coast, in the Bay of Fundy, off Nantucket shoals, and occasionally even on the dangerous and dreaded Georges Bank, one hundred miles east of Cape Cod. This Bank with its swift and heavy tides was held to be so perilous that for generations fishermen did not dare cast their anchors in its waters and used only drift-fishing to obtain their catch.

For two centuries and more after their first voyage to the Grand Banks, Massachusetts fishermen in particular so distinguished themselves by their hardihood and industry that they and their vessels became known far and wide. Only five years after they had made their first venture they had 665 vessels there and over 4000 fishermen and were drawing from the sea annually some 400,000 quintals of cod, which, since a quintal is 112 pounds, means around 50,000,000 pounds of fish.

Throughout the world there is probably no

one area of ocean which equals either in historic interest or in economic importance these Grand Banks of Newfoundland. Known for untold years to foreign vessels, as we have seen, they began now at the close of the seventeenth century to be the goal of countless New England fishermen. Here over a vast expanse of gray, cold seas, swept by fogs and menaced by icebergs, over an area the size of

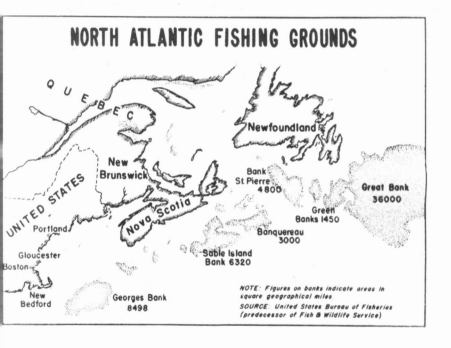

NORTH ATLANTIC FISHING GROUNDS

QUEBEC

Newfoundland

New Brunswick

UNITED STATES

Portland

Nova Scotia

Gloucester

Boston

New Bedford

Georges Bank
8498

Sable Island
Bank 6320

Bank
St Pierre
4800

Banquereau
3000

Green
Banks 1450

Great Bank
36000

NOTE: Figures on banks indicate areas in square geographical miles
SOURCE: United States Bureau of Fisheries (predecessor of Fish & Wildlife Service)

the state of Indiana, men and boys from Cape
Cod and Cape Ann, from Boston, Scituate,
Duxbury, Marblehead, Beverly, Salem, Ips-
wich, and Gloucester, began to drop their lines
above those submerged tablelands or sub-
marine plateaus known as "banks." Here the
water is more shallow than in open ocean, its
depth varying from 50 to 400 feet; and here
as in no other place or for so long a time during
the year, the cod swim in incredible numbers
since they prefer the rocky, pebbly, or sandy
bottoms provided off Newfoundland. The fishing season then as now was at its best from
April to October. Stout, well-manned vessels
could and did often make three trips a season.
Beginning in early spring, they sailed northward in rude ballast, and returned with their
holds laden with well-salted fish.

Thus, long before a hundred years had
passed after the permanent settlement of New
England, the energy, courage, and labor of
her fishermen had built up an industry which
was to be, indeed had already come to be by

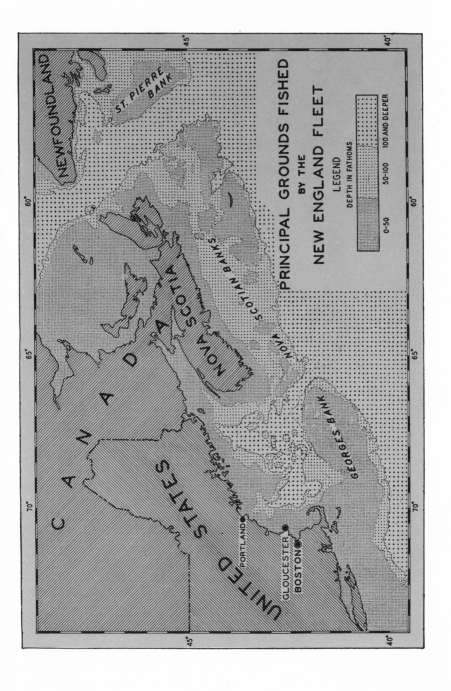

PRINCIPAL GROUNDS FISHED
BY THE
NEW ENGLAND FLEET

LEGEND
DEPTH IN FATHOMS

0-50   50-100   100 AND DEEPER

the turn of the seventeenth into the eighteenth century, the very backbone of colonial America. New England fishermen quickly outdid those of the mother country both in quantity and in quality just as they surpassed those from the Canadian-French settlements in spite of bitter rivalry and even warfare. What this early enterprise meant to our country in terms of its foreign trade, how it unquestionably was to result in the establishment of our famous merchant marine of the eighteenth and nineteenth centuries, we shall see in the next chapter.

3

Fishermen and Early American Trade

WHEN CAPTAIN John Smith in 1614 sent 40,000 dried cod to Spain in one of his ships which had been fishing off Monhegan Island, he was not doing anything unusual even at that early date. Fish had been carried for at least a hundred years from the seas off Labrador and Newfoundland to the ports of England, Spain, France, and Portugal. Foreign countries needed them as food and especially those largely Catholic countries where fish-eating days were prescribed by the Church.

New England skippers of fishing vessels were not slow in following his good example. Whether they themselves piloted their boats

across the Atlantic or whether Boston merchants bought their catch and sent it forth
under the charge of other mariners is not easy
to discover from the all too scant records of

our colonial trading. The fishermen of New England have never been by nature "deep water" sailors. Their fishing grounds rather than foreign ports have been their goals.

An early sixteenth-century shipbuilding scene

Yet whoever may have manned our first trading ships, their high, rounded bows were surely cutting through home and foreign waters long before the seventeenth century came to a close. Shipbuilding began as early as 1631 with the launching of Governor John Winthrop's *Blessing of the Bay*. By 1660 it had become a leading industry in a dozen New England ports, among them Salem, Gloucester, Medford, Portsmouth, and, of course, Boston. These first American ships were small affairs enough in comparison with those to be built during the following two centuries. Few of them could carry more than thirty tons of cargo; few were over fifty feet in length. Nevertheless they managed to reach not only the ports of New York, Chesapeake Bay, and Virginia, but Lisbon, Bilboa, Marseilles, and Calais as well. And in addition to the fish which crammed their holds, they early began to carry lumber, barrels, staves for Spanish wine casks, and even stout timbers on their narrow decks. The forests of Maine supplied

these timbers as masts for the British Royal
Navy of King Charles II, who came to the
English throne in 1660. We know upon the
good authority of the famous English diarist

The *Mayflower II* under construction

Samuel Pepys that in the year 1666 "four ships from New England" brought such mighty tree trunks to the port of Falmouth in Dorsetshire.

Nor did these first New England ships, which kept increasing in size as their cargoes increased in nature and value, sail homeward empty of wealth. In exchange for fish and lumber they brought tobacco from Virginia; coffee from Brazil; salt from Cadiz in Spain; wine from the Madeira Islands; and oranges and grapes from Malaga and Valencia to lend excitement to New England dinner tables.

In these colonial days the West Indies provided the most ready market for New England dried, or salted, or pickled fish. Although the most superior quality of the catch was taken to France and Spain, the islands of Jamaica and Barbados willingly received the lower grades. From these tropical islands our ships brought home molasses and sugar cane for the making of New England rum, and from Honduras fragrant woods for the adornment of the homes of Boston merchants.

Construction of the Pilgrim shallop
that was built in 1957 to serve the *Mayflower II*

It is not difficult, then, to see how important
and even invaluable to our earliest American
economy were the fish and the men who
caught them. Without both we should hardly
have survived as a small people on the eastern
fringe of a vast, unknown country, the explo-
ration and settlement of which were not to
begin for another hundred years. The lowly

The Pilgrim shallop with the hull nearly completed

codfish and his daring captors were responsible for the shipbuilding in which, after the Revolutionary War and in the century following, we were to excel all other nations, just as both were responsible for our first ventures in trade, which was eventually to extend to the four corners of the earth and make American ships and seamen known throughout the world.

The shallop rigged and ready to be launched

When we remember these things and ac-
cord to our fishermen the gratitude and honor
which they so richly deserve, we are more than
a little surprised to realize that as a group of
people they did not contribute largely to sea-
manship as a profession. After our foreign
trade had become firmly established, after
larger ships had been designed and built by

Another view of the shallop.
This is the type of boat the Pilgrims
would have used for fishing.

New England and New York marine architects
and shipwrights, when, after the Revolution
had given us our independence as a nation,
American ships began to carry our products to
far shores, to East India, China, and the South
Sea Islands, fishermen with rare exceptions
were not numbered either among their crews
or among their officers and commanders.

There seem to be several reasons for this somewhat singular truth — reasons which in themselves characterize our fishermen and in a sense separate them from other men who have followed the seas.

In the first place, they were a notably independent sort of people. They did not take kindly to the rigid discipline exacted from the crew of a great ship engaged in foreign trade. They liked, instead, to do things "on their own hook," a phrase which originated among them and which referred both to provisions supplied by each man among the small crew of a fishing vessel and to the method of payment on such a vessel, whereby a man was paid according to the number of fish he caught "on his own hook."

The very hardships and dangers which they endured on their trips to the Banks, or to nearer waters; the initiative and quick decisions demanded of them; the sense of comradeship which a crew of six or eight men engendered by their life together on a relatively

small craft — all these made them unwilling to labor as ordinary seamen among many other sailors on a great East Indiaman or, later, on a clipper ship. They did not like to take orders. They preferred to be "on their own."

Nor did they as a class of men and boys care for long voyages to foreign lands. After their six months of rigorous toil they liked to stay at home for the remainder of the year. Most New England fishermen were farmers as well, in a small way. They could rest from their work during the winter months, though many of them went to home fishing grounds for a few days now and again. They could repair their boats and gear, plant their few acres in the spring, and leave the care of them to wives and children after they had sailed away with a score of other friendly boats from their own ports — boats and crews with whom they often stayed in touch off Labrador or Newfoundland.

There was a camaraderie in fishing. The men engaged in it had a society all their own, rude perhaps, but understanding and kind.

illiam B. Phillips of Swampscott, Mass.

Democracy was at its best and noblest off those foggy northern coasts. How vividly Kipling describes this in Chapter 8 of *Captains Courageous!* We watch the boats of the Gloucester fleet arriving until nearly a hundred vessels from there and elsewhere are riding at anchor not far from the dreaded Virgin Rocks. We hear the bantering pleasantries called across the water from one deck to another, the good-natured insults, the questions about the folks at home, about the "best girls" waiting there for their

Aboard a fishing schooner catching mackerel with a seine

young men to return. Swedes and Portuguese, Irish and Canadian French, Newfoundlanders and boys from Maine, skippers and cooks alike — all exchange old jokes and recall former incidents. In the gale at night all stand ready to pull up any dory lost in the fog and wind and to give the hospitality of their crowded, reeking cabins to any drenched and bewildered fisherman who could not reach his own vessel.

The typical fisherman's son looked forward to following his father's way of life. Intelligent though he usually was, he was not often inclined to be bookish as were many of the New England boys who worked up from cabin boy and ordinary seaman to an officer's status in the ships of the merchant marine and finally to a captain's command. His ambitions may not have been so high as theirs, but he had, like them, the sea in his blood. Newfoundland to him looked far better than Canton or Calcutta, and his father's tossing boat a more congenial home than the forecastle of a great ship.

Even at nine or ten years of age he might well be taken along by his father, or by some uncle, or older brother. He was often at that age a cook for the crew, tending the tiny open fireplace, which before the days of stoves on fishing vessels was situated at the end of the stuffy single cabin. After he had fed his tired shipmates on hardtack and salt beef and the odds and ends of fish, often made into a chowder from evaporated canned milk, he could listen to their yarns and get the "feel" of their rough and dangerous life.

And, of course, he learned early to drop lines on his own and by the age of fifteen or sixteen had often become an accomplished fisherman. Such young boys were known as "cut-tails" from the pieces they snipped from the tails of the cod which they caught. A cut-tail received no wages from his work on board except payment for the few fish he actually caught in his odd hours.

The New England fisherman, in point of fact, portrays for the most part a curious anomaly, or puzzle. In a certain way the most stalwart of men in the sense that he pursued the most tough and hazardous of callings, his rugged independence seemingly discouraged his participation in larger, more far-flung enterprises. Nor did he, as a rule, possess the financial means for uncertain and probably uncongenial investments. He was self-respecting, often poor, yet proud of his capacity to do hard, gruelling work and to cope with danger and perhaps disaster. When the Great West was opened by our pioneers, he was rarely among those leaving home for new lands and fortunes. When great factories began to be opened in the nineteenth century along our swift rivers, he was not likely to be among their workers, deciding instead to stick to his small house, his fishing boat, and his few acres in Marblehead, or Gloucester, or Salem, or on some Maine bay or island.

His one ambition and desire was to catch fish. And perhaps in the long view of our history, it is most fortunate that he was precisely the manner of man that he was!

Captain Dolison of the schooner *Genesta*

4

The Ways and Methods of Fishing

IN ANY description of fishing as it has been carried on for more than three centuries by our New England fishing fleets, the first thing necessary to picture in our minds is, of course, the vessels which comprised these fleets. What manner of boats did our colonial fishermen sail in New England waters and after a few years to the Grand Banks of Newfoundland? I shall try to answer this question in as simple and nontechnical language as possible, hoping that the illustrations given will help my readers to visualize our earliest attempts at building boats for our earliest and most essential industry.

One may well think that the Indians, who taught the first settlers many things, might well have given them some ideas about sailing, but, as a matter of fact, Indians seem to have been sadly lacking in their knowledge of the sea and in any attempt whatever to venture far from the safety of its shores. Their birch-bark canoes evidently closely hugged the land, and they themselves were in no sense sailors or even fishermen except when need made the netting or hooking of fish imperative. Our New England forefathers quite clearly depended on the mother country for their first adventures in the framing of ships, nor were their plans for these different in most respects from those to which they or their forebears had been accustomed in European waters.

Our colonial fishing boats, that is those constructed and sailed in the seventeenth century were, as we have seen, small, not often over fifty feet in length and capable of carrying only some twenty to thirty tons of cargo. They were often made by our early fishermen or by men skillful at ship carpentry in barns or sheds during the winter season and then hauled to the shore by oxen over the last of the snow for their launching in the spring. We unfortunately know far more about the beds, chairs, and tables constructed for colonial homes than we know about our first boats; in fact, it is difficult from lack of accurate information to discover precisely what these fishing vessels were like. Nor are there many pictures of them before the nineteenth century.

In the Peabody Museum in Salem, however, there is a model of the ketch *Sparrow Hawk*, which brought forty passengers from England in the year 1626 and which probably was very similar to most of our first boats used in fishing. These ketches were rounded at both ends, the keel curving upward toward bow and stern. They were some nine or ten feet deep in their holds and required only seven or eight feet of water for draught. They had single decks, one mast amidships with a square sail and often a mast nearer the stern which carried a triangular

The *Sparrow Hawk*

or lateen sail of the type still commonly seen on Mediterranean craft. Such round-bottomed boats as these, unseaworthy as they would seem today, apparently rode the waves well. At all events, the *Sparrow Hawk* weathered the Atlantic safely, only to be wrecked on Cape Cod!

The year 1713 really marks the first radical change in the construction of fishing vessels. In that year, Cape Ann men will tell you, a certain Captain Andrew Robinson of Gloucester masted and rigged a ketch after a new fashion. He did away with the square mainsail, substituted fore and aft sails, and used such sails not only on two masts, a main and a fore, but invented a jibsail as well, at the bow. The characterization of his craft, which he called a *schooner*, seems to have come from the New England colloquial term "scoon," which originally meant the swift skipping of a stone across water. His new rigging resulted in such speed that, in the opinion of those who watched the launching of his boat, it caused her to "scoon"; hence, the story goes, he seized upon the name for his vessel and lived to hear it used for all boats masted and rigged after the manner of his invention.

The schooner *Hannah* in 1775. She was America's first regularly commissioned warship.

In the eighteenth century, after the Revolution, a distinctly American craft known as the *chebacco* boat because it was built in the parish of Chebacco, now a part of the town of Essex, came into general use in fishing. These differed little from ketches except for their sharper sterns. After the War of 1812 a boat called a *pinky* seems to have been in high favor among our fishermen, especially among those in Maine

A drawing made in 1836 of a chebacco boat

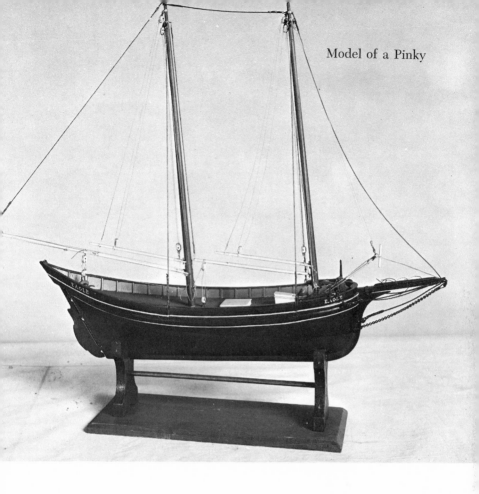

where many pinkies were built. It gained its name from its so-called "pink," which was a V-shaped wooden structure erected at the stern to serve as a rest for the long boom of the mainmast.

Although chebacco boats and pinkies continued to be built and sailed throughout the eighteenth and well into the nineteenth century, Captain Robinson's schooner meant a revolution in our fishing craft. Changes and innovations were gradually made in the shape of hulls and in the arrangement of decks. Sterns became wider and less rounded, bows sharper and narrower, decks longer and more broad, cargo capacity deeper. In many schooners the aft, or quarter, deck was so raised above the main deck that the vessel was known as a "heel-tapper," since this quarter-deck resembled the heel of an inverted shoe. In stormy weather when the main deck might well be washed by the sea the crew often fished from this high quarter-deck.

Living accommodations on fishing vessels until late in the nineteenth century continued to be crowded and primitive. The cabin, placed aft below the quarter-deck, had bunks around the sides and a board table in the center. A rude fireplace, built of brick or stone and situated at the after end of the cabin,

The schooner *Raven* in 1801. Note the high quarterdeck.

served both for heating and cooking, the smoke escaping as best it could through a chimney in the cabin roof, as Kipling describes in *Captains Courageous.*

In the last decades of the nineteenth century fishing schooners became still longer and deeper, able to carry double their earlier tonnage, capable also of more auxiliary sail, sharper in outline, at once more graceful and more swift. One of these deserving special mention was the *Grampus,* designed and built in 1886 for the United States Fish Commission.

Captain Robinson's basic plan, however, prevailed, together

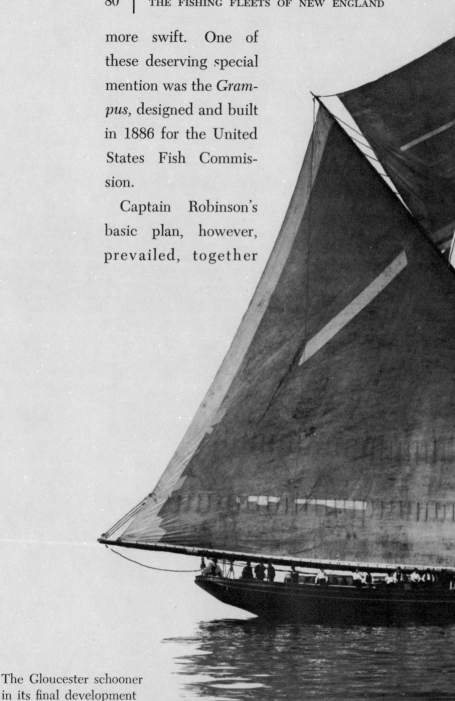

The Gloucester schooner in its final development

with his name for his vessel. Schooners such boats have continued to be, whether engaged in fishing off Newfoundland or in carrying lumber from Nova Scotian and Maine ports to southern harbors. Their form and rigging have influenced the designs of our modern yachts and sloops and are still predominant in the so-called "windjammers," which now sail on pleasure cruises along the Maine coast in the summer.

And Gloucester, having by the early nineteenth century risen to prominence above all other fishing towns, still treasures with pride the name of their inventor, even in these days when engines have all but driven sails from the seas.

The oldest method of fishing for cod, a method without doubt employed by Breton and Basque fishermen in those dim, unrecorded years even before the sixteenth century, was hand-lining from the deck. For over two hundred years our New England fishermen caught their fish in this way. It meant simply that every man not on watch, with the usual exception of the cook and the skipper, dropped his line either from the port or starboard side of the vessel into water anywhere from fifty to a hundred and fifty feet in depth. Each line was weighted by a lead, or sinker, varying in weight from three to five pounds.

Cod are groundfish, swimming close to the bottom of the sea, and long, heavily weighted lines were necessary in hand-line fishing. There were usually two hooks on each line, though some fishermen preferred to handle two one-hook lines. The hooks were baited with shucked clams brought along in tubs for the purpose, or pieces of herring or mackerel about an inch square, or with capelin whenever these small fish, which were found in vast schools and which were popular with cod, could be caught in dip-nets.

On some vessels, especially in the earliest years of fishing off the Banks, an outboard

staging was built along the sides, and each
fisherman stood in half a barrel, or hogshead,
placed on this staging. This protected him
from the wash of the sea in rough weather and
lent him some support for his line. When the
fish were "running" well, he often hooked two
at once, a heavy load to haul to the surface
since there are records of cod weighing from
fifty to a hundred pounds. Even the usual
weight of ten to fifteen pounds was not incon-
siderable to draw up through deep water.

Once the fish were hauled up to the side of
the boat, they were "slatted" off the hook by
a deft movement (unless their voracious swal-
lowing of it made "slatting" impossible!) and
thrown into tubs placed just behind the fishermen. There were various means of counting
them, each fisherman being responsible for his
own count, an important matter to him since
on the share system he was paid for his actual
catch. On some vessels the tongues were im-
mediately cut out to serve as a tally, or the
tail fin was severed; on others the busy skipper,

An early
diagrammatic
view of
hand-lining

hurrying along his decks, carefully recorded each man's catch on a board kept for that purpose with every name set down.

Such hand-line fishing from the deck meant a gruelling day's work. The crew were routed from their bunks at earliest dawn and after a hasty breakfast took their places at the low deck railings, or bulwarks, whatever the weather. The number of men depended, of course, upon the size of the vessel. Some fishing boats carried only eight or ten men; others, as the size of the vessels increased, had double that number. Two men served on the two-hour watches, one at the wheel when the ship was under way, the other in the lookout at the bow or in the crow's-nest upon the mast. Fishing continued throughout the day with time out only for dinner or for an occasional "mug-up" of bread or hardtack with coffee. When fish grew scarce or nonexistent in one locality, the anchor was hauled up and the boat moved on to another.

In the late afternoon or sometimes, on days

Hand-lining on the banks

of prime fishing, at night by the light of lanterns, the sorting and cleaning of the fish began. Fishermen might well be drenched to the skin and tired to the point of exhaustion, their hands bruised and cut by taut lines or by sharp, barbed hooks, their backs and legs cruelly aching; but they expected, and got, no time for rest. Their fish must be cared for at once, else their trip to the Banks was a costly failure.

They worked in groups of three, known as "dressing gangs," at the cleaning. One man called a "throater" cut off the heads; a second, the "gutter," disemboweled the bellies, throwing the entrails over the side; a third, the "splitter," cut out the backbone with his sharp, curved splitting-knife, a skillful operation which demanded great care and dexterity. The three stood by a small table or bench necessary to their work and with almost in-

credible rapidity passed the cod from one to another. The "gutter" was careful to save the liver from his refuse material. This he threw into the "liver butt." Cod liver oil was valuable in itself since it was sold in those days, not for medicinal purposes, but to saddlers and tanners eager to get it for use on leather.

Once the gutted and split fish were soaked clean in tubs of salt water, they were pitched

dressing gang at work

into the hold of the vessel where they were piled and packed by the "salters," who covered layers of them with generous scoops of salt. Sometimes young boys began their apprenticeship as future fishermen by acting as "salters' devils," working in the stuffy, reeking hold at filling baskets with salt for the packers.

When, often late at night, the day's toil was over, the fishermen crawled into their cabin

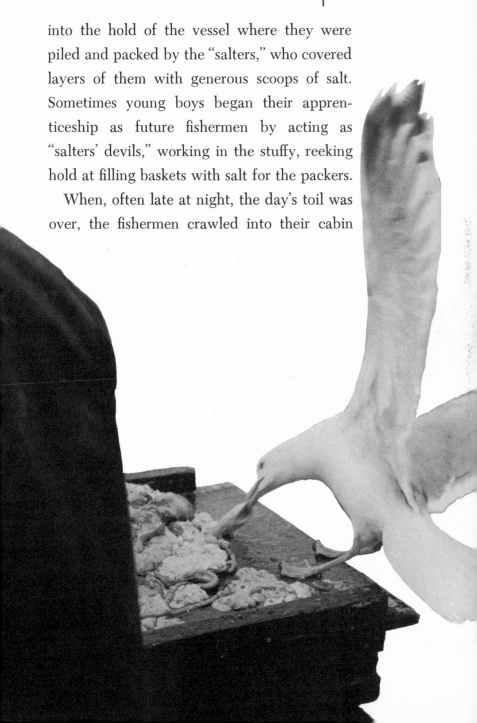

bunks, relying on the heat from their bodies to dry out their wet clothing, knowing that in a few hours the call would come to be up and doing once again. In *Captains Courageous* Dan Troop, the skipper's son, asks Harvey Cheyne, the rescued castaway from the great liner, what in Harvey's opinion is the thing most desired by a fisherman upon his return home. Harvey, not unreasonably, ventures the guess of a hot bath; but Dan assures him that a dry nightshirt is better than anything else in the world. His mother will have one ready for him in Gloucester, Dan says, and he can hardly wait to get within its clean, freshly ironed folds and go to sleep!

Early in the nineteenth century fishing craft began to carry dories to the Banks and to do their hand-line fishing from these rather than from the deck of the main vessel. Skippers proved right in their assumption that two men in a dory could catch more fish, largely because the dories could move easily and swiftly from one fishing ground to another and thus cover a larger area of ocean. These dories were some thirteen feet in length and, as all sailors know, have always been the most seaworthy of small boats. The number of dories carried, piled upside down on the tops of the cabins and lashed securely there, depended upon the size of the fishing vessel. Larger craft carried as many as ten or twelve; smaller ones, four or six.

Men and boys in dories used the same gear and technique in actual fishing as they had used from the deck of the schooner, or pinky, or chebacco boat. At dawn they rowed away from the home vessel, one eastward, another westward, yet another north or south, often crossing a mile or more of sea. Tossed about on the waves in brisk weather, frequently enveloped by fog, they dropped their own anchors wherever the fish were biting and put in a day's hard work on their own.

A dory of ordinary length could hold and carry some 1700 pounds of fish, and it was the hope of both men fishing that they could bring back a capacity load in the late afternoon. Although some dories carried a com-

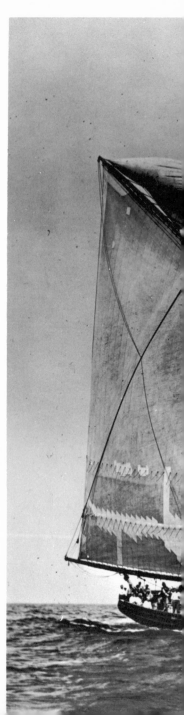

A Gloucester schooner with its nests of dories

pass, men often found it difficult, especially in fog, to determine the anchorage of the parent ship since winds, upon which they depended for the general direction, were given to sudden shifting. Fishing vessels engaged in hand-line dory fishing sometimes carried a

swivel gun which the skipper fired in foggy weather to call in his dories. On fair, clear days he relied upon a horn or the pealing of a bell, upon a bushel basket which he hoisted on the mast, or merely upon himself aloft in the main rigging and swinging his hat!

A fishing dory with the trawls

The most important form of fishing, the one that gave honor and eminence to our fleets and meant the heyday of their adventuresome history under sail, was that of laying and hauling trawls. This method, at once heroic, dangerous, and extremely profitable, prevailed off the Banks (and in home waters as well) from around 1850 until the invention and widespread use of the gasoline engine early in our present century revolutionized the tenor and the tempo of our lives, both on land and sea. Even today trawling has not entirely disappeared. Small boats and single fishermen still set and haul trawls off our coasts; and although such fishing has virtually passed away from the Grand Banks, a tiny percentage of Canadian fishermen, unable financially to procure engines and gear, even now employ this method of catching fish in their teeming waters.

What, then, was and is a trawl? It is a stout cord line, sometimes a mile or more in length, which at every six feet or so is hung with another line smaller in size and about three feet long. At the end of each of these shorter lines is a weighted hook. In the years devoted by our fishing fleets to dory trawling such trawls were neatly coiled in tubs made from barrels or casks long before the vessel reached the fishing grounds. This conglomeration of lines and hooks required care, and first-class skippers always saw to it that all should be in readiness by the time their vessels with their piled dories, one stowed away in another, arrived at the places for fishing.

Then the baiting of the trawls began. This meant unwinding the trawl from the tub, baiting each hook, and coiling the long cord line again in the half-barrel, or trawl tub. When the actual fishing began at dawn, in almost any weather except the most monstrous of gales, the trawl tubs were placed in the dories, usually two to four to each dory. With them, in addition to a jug of fresh water, some food, and a mast and sail in case of trouble while away from the parent vessel, were also placed two anchors and two buoys. The buoys, usually casks or small barrels called trawl buoys, were to mark the beginning and the end of the trawl; the anchors were to hold the buoys in place and to keep the trawl, once it was laid on the bottom of the sea.

As in hand-line fishing two men manned each dory, one to row and the other to uncoil the baited trawls and fling them into the sea. When they were set, if the cod were plentiful,

Sharpening
the hooks
on a trawl

the men almost at once started back along the length of the trawl lines, one man hauling up the trawl and the other coiling it. In the bow of each dory was a broad wheel called a "gurdy." When fishing for halibut the trawl line was run over the gurdy as it was pulled aboard. The fish on the hooks were freed by quick yanks and twists of the short, hooked lines and thrown into the wide bottom of the dory. In times of busy hauling the oarsman shipped his oars, depended upon the trawl itself to keep his boat in position, and began to rebait the hooks, and to coil the lines again in an empty tub so that they would be ready for another setting.

Fishermen engaged in this job were of necessity strong and plucky fellows. There could hardly be more tough work in any calling than moving across a rough sea all day long, setting and hauling trawls from a rocking dory. Even on fair, still days, and there were many in the summer months, the very glare and heat of the sun were hard on eyes and exposed skin.

Not a moment of rest or relaxation was possible except as time was taken for a hurried lunch either on the parent vessel, if she were close enough at hand, or in the dory itself.

Initiative and quick decisions, care in keeping one's balance, constant watchfulness — all were imperative. If the hooks brought up, as they often did, other fish than the cod, these were thrown back into the sea unless they, too, possessed marketable value. It was cod which the trawl fishermen were seeking; and as the dory filled with flapping, panting fish, lying ever lower in the water as it did so, they forgot their weariness and danger. To be called "a high-liner," which meant the best of Bank fishermen, was their ambition; and dories heaped with fish were one of the requirements for gaining that distinction and meriting that term. One recalls how proud Harvey Cheyne felt when he was allowed to man a dory with Dan Troop and to haul in the heavy trawls. We recall, too, with a shudder the dead Frenchman whom they hauled up on one of their hooks as they fished off the Virgin Rocks!

Baiting a trawl

Darkness often fell over the ocean before all the dories had returned to the vessel. On occasion the skipper sailed about to pick them up, especially if there were fog or if the wind rose suddenly. There are far too many stories of strayed dories, sometimes rescued by other vessels, sometimes not picked up at all, for with all its hardy qualities as a fishing boat a laden dory might well be a frail craft in the worst of weather.

Once the trawlers had made the vessel, hoisted their dories to her deck and pitched their catch aboard, the endless toil of cleaning began — the throating, gutting, and splitting. No matter how long the day at the trawls had been, the inevitable attention to the catch must be accomplished by the same tired fishermen. Yet with all its hazards and its toils this trawling for cod from open dories has always remained the most interesting and the bravest form of fishing in its long history.

Only a few weeks ago in Gloucester I met an old fisherman who remembered his boy-

The day's catch

hood in 1890, when, only ten years old, he went with his father to the Grand Banks. He was far too young then to go out in a dory, being allowed only to drop his line from the deck of the schooner during the hours when the dories were far afloat. But he told me

Preparing the trawl

proudly that he caught 1000 cod on his own even at that age, and more proudly that at fifteen he could manage a dory and a trawl as well as the next man.

"The plain fact is," he said, "that I was a high-liner by the time I was seventeen. Fishing is tame enough in these days. It can't make boys into men as it used to do when I was young. There's nothing like a dory adrift on a high sea to make a shaver grow up into something stout and strong. Take it from me, lady! I learned to be a fisherman in the hard way, not on one of these pleasure cruisers that they call fishing boats today."

The old fisherman was right in more ways than one. Fishing today is not what it was in his youth or in that of Harvey Cheyne and Dan Troop. The "pleasure cruisers" to which he so bitterly referred are the otter trawlers, which, beginning with the year 1905, were to alter beyond all recognition the ways and methods of our earlier New England fishing fleets.

In that critical year the first otter trawler, called *The Spray*, sailed under steam out of Boston for the Banks of Newfoundland; a few years later six such vessels were steaming out of the same harbor; by 1925 there was an

The steam trawler *Coot* built in 1919

almost countless number of these new trawlers equipped with gasoline engines instead of steam. Each of these swift and heavy boats carried an otter trawl or sometimes two.

An otter trawl is a conical bag of heavy netting designed to be lowered from the vessel and dragged across the bottom of the sea. It derives its name from two so-called "otter boards," which are attached to the two towing cables in such a way that the resistance of the water causes the boards to pull away from each other and thus to keep the mouth of the net open. These otter boards resemble doors of average size and are, indeed, sometimes called "otter doors." An averagely large otter trawler net is about 150 feet long, and it is capable of hauling in from 3000 to 5000 pounds of fish in a tow of about an hour, provided it is towed or dragged across sea bottoms where fish are plentiful. The cables of coiled wire which drag the net are operated over engine-run winches.

Perhaps the old man was more than a little

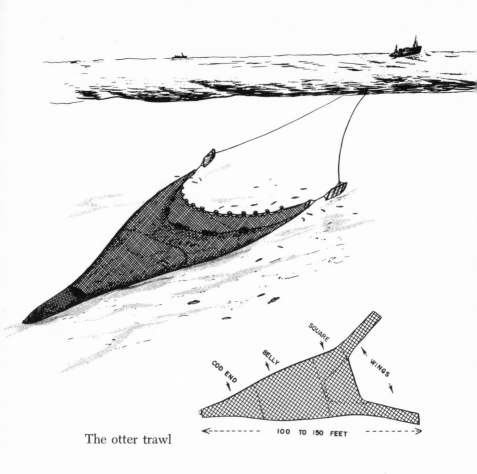

The otter trawl

COD END BELLY SQUARE WINGS

100 TO 150 FEET

bitter and ironical in terming such a craft a "pleasure cruiser," for fishing from an otter trawler still demands long hours of hard work in manipulating the great net, keeping it in repair — for it is constantly becoming torn — and handling the vast quantity of fish which

it drags up from the bottom of the sea. Even
with the refrigeration which such trawlers now
carry, the life of men on board hardly resem-
bles a cruise merely for pleasure.

Nevertheless it is undeniably true that otter
trawling has not only changed radically all the
old methods of fishing, but has made sad in-
roads upon the individuality and independence
of the New England fisherman. From being
entirely "on his own hook" as in former years,
he must now co-operate in a mechanized industry. What such trawlers have meant and
are meaning to fishing as a part of our economic life, both in terms of profit and of loss,
we shall see in another chapter.

Fishermen today on otter trawlers are sure
of good and fresh food. They no longer have
to rely on hardtack, salted beef, baked beans,
or chowders made with evaporated milk and
odds and ends of fish. They are sure now, too,
of dry and decent bunks. The trawler can
afford to wait for fairly good weather on the
fishing grounds since nets are not often

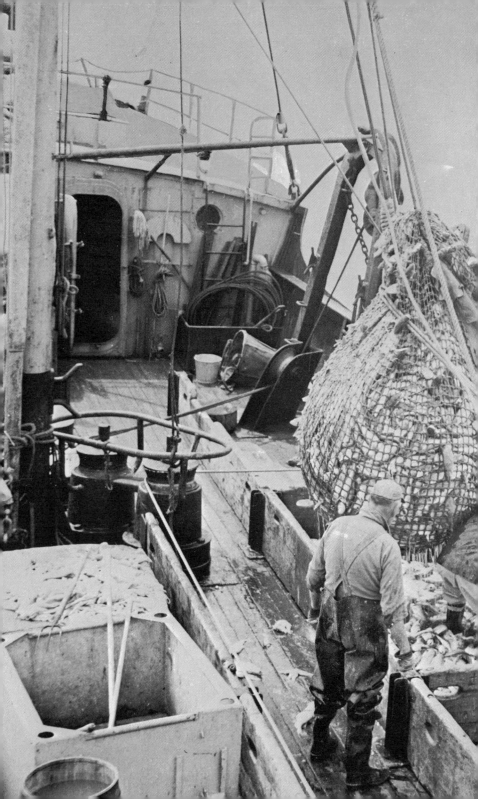

dropped into rough seas. Radio equipment and even radar now eliminate most of the old perils. Lines with their sharp, baited hooks are for the most part things of the past just as are wet clothes, hunger and terror, long, uncertain days, and uncertain rewards. Men on such trawlers, even though some of their many possible trips each year are less successful than others, are assured of more money in view of the stupendous number of fish caught.

The "cod end" of a trawl
with its load of fish
being hauled aboard

They are also assured, in case of breakdown of the trawler on any given trip, a daily wage in addition to their actual living expenses.

Without doubt there is more than an element of truth in the old fisherman's comment. Our former fishing fleets have gone past all recall. The sails of nearly one hundred vessels of every possible make and build — sails which Harvey Cheyne, seeing them from the deck of the *We're Here* as the rising sun brought out all their hues, knew he would never forget — will not again be seen either in the waters off Newfoundland or on our home fishing grounds.

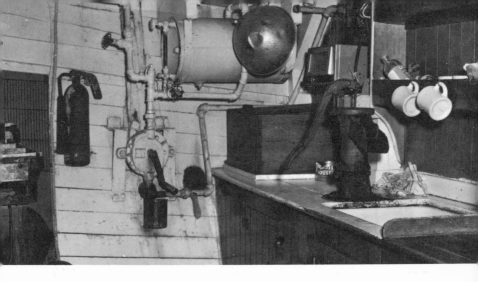

Below decks on a modern fishing vessel

Today, diesel engines push their boats northward, independent of wind and weather,
making the nine hundred miles to Newfoundland in a fraction of the time required by
Captain Andrew Robinson's first schooner and
the ones which followed her. But it is ques-
tionable whether these new boats produce
many human beings like Disko Troop and
Manuel, the Portuguese, or boys like Dan or
like Harvey Cheyne once he had learned to
value the character of men more than money
or than private railroad trains.

An ancient Greek poet once wrote that to a

brave man danger has glory in its face. Whether our New England fishermen for three centuries agreed with him, of whom they had probably never heard, we shall never know; but it is certain that

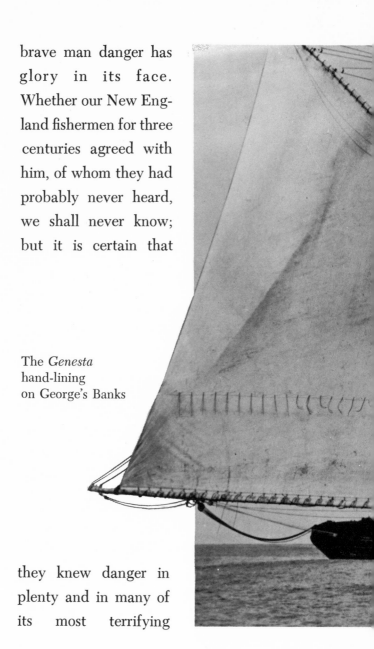

The *Genesta*
hand-lining
on George's Banks

they knew danger in plenty and in many of its most terrifying

forms. In homage to them let us now learn about some of the perils which they so gallantly weathered as they sailed northward from our fishing ports toward the gray, relentless seas of Newfoundland.

5

The Dangers in a Fisherman's Life

THE MOST interesting as well as most typical period in the story of our New England fishing fleets was that span of time between 1850 and 1920. The former date marked the approximate beginning of trawl fishing from dories; the latter, the equally approximate time for the ousting of the dory-laden sailing schooner by the power-driven otter trawler. Within these seventy years, during which the fishing for cod off the banks of Newfoundland reached the height of its importance as an industry under sail, three generations of New England men and boys knew well all those dangers which made the fisherman's calling one of endurance, hardihood, and courage.

The weather was, of course, the most formid-
able of their adversaries, just as it might be the
most gracious of their friends. Storms and high
winds, sudden squalls of snow and sleet, north-

Piled up on the rocks of Cape Anne

east gales blowing sometimes for days on end
were constantly taking their toll of men and
ships. The records of the port of Gloucester
alone bear generous witness to such bitter loss.

In the years between 1830 and 1873, 281 vessels of its fleet were lost with 1252 men aboard them. One mighty gale on February 24, 1862, cost 15 schooners and 120 men and resulted in 70 Gloucester widows and 140 fatherless children.

Nor were such storms confined to far northern waters. In August, 1873, cruel tides on the shoals of the dreaded Georges Bank claimed

The *Gertrude L. Thebaud*
in heavy weather

nine Gloucester vessels and 128 fishermen; and in all such storms, of course, other New England ports were shattered by similar sorrows. When the fleets left for the waters off Newfoundland in the spring and the church bells of a hundred harbors rang out their best wishes and their good cheer, the women and the children gathered at the piers knew all too well that the same bells might be tolling sad tidings a few months later.

Ice, especially in the early spring when the floes and bergs floated down from the Arctic, was a dire menace. When one recalls the fate of the *Titanic* in 1912 and the proud boast of her officers that God Himself could not sink her, one can more easily imagine the disaster lying in wait for a small fishing vessel, which, if it struck even a large cake of floating ice in a heavy sea, might well be instantly cut into pieces. Ice and consequent cold meant as well frozen sails to reef and frozen ropes to handle, not to mention frostbitten, useless fingers and toes, or the brittle coat which under such conditions sheathed the schooner from stem to stern and made any movement on board her of peril to all from skipper to crew.

Fog was a danger dreaded by all fishermen, especially the men and boys who manned the

The end of the voyage

dories; and Grand Banks fog, deeper, darker, and more persistent than any known to sailors, was always seemingly lying in wait with its stealthy, blinding folds. Such fog might well cut off all marks to guide a dory back to the parent ship and leave two men alone, afloat on a measureless, empty, often invisible sea. It meant wearisome journeys spent in continual labor at the oars, days and nights without food or water, despair growing hourly as the gray obscurity deepened, shutting out all knowledge of position or of place. There are countless records of such dories "lost in fog" as their men rowed on and on, hoping against hope to reach some unknown shore or to be rescued by some vessel not their own which might provide at least a temporary haven from exhaustion, hunger, and fear.

In the late nineteenth and early twentieth centuries ocean liners, then unequipped with modern devices such as radar, threatened all fishing craft. Out of the darkness or fog their great bulks loomed above the small, tossing

A sinking dragger

vessels, prophesying almost certain destruction. The tragic truth of such disaster came home to me when in late April of 1913 I crossed the Atlantic from Montreal to Liverpool, steaming for the first few days through the fog-swept waters of the Gulf of St. Lawrence, as we skirted the south coast of Newfoundland.

One night, when we were passing through the fishing grounds off Cape Race, I awoke to the perceptible slowing of our ship, then to the stilling of our engines, and to the constant bellowing of our foghorn. At breakfast the steward told me that we had struck and sunk a fishing schooner and that in the hope of rescuing her crew we had lowered boats and done all that we could.

"Which was precisely nothing," the steward said. "Those poor fellows haven't the ghost of a chance when they get in our course, God help them!"

Back from the Banks in wintertime

There were many other dangers in a fisherman's life, less tragic, to be sure, than storms, ice, fog, and collision, but still terrifying in themselves and in their consequences. Illness from cold and exposure were common anxieties as were accidents of all sorts from falling from rigging or on slippery decks to drowning, from infection often resulting in painful abscesses or boils, known in fisherman's language as "gurry sores," to burns from pots of scalding coffee suddenly overturned by a quick pitch of the vessel in a high sea.

Fish themselves might sometimes be the source of peril and even of disaster. Sharks were common enemies, especially in fairly shallow water; and although in New England or Newfoundland waters they were more eager for a meal of fish than of human flesh, they could well be dangerous as they lounged about a laden dory.

Halibut could also give a great deal of trouble. When two dory fishermen found a hundred-and-fifty-pound halibut instead of a ten-pound cod on one of their trawl hooks, they knew they were in for a lively half-hour of battle which might well result in a capsized dory. And even when the great gray creature had at last been hauled over the careening side, he might still continue to show his fury by mighty poundings of his head and tail until some blows from a "gobstick" finally silenced him before he had damaged the dory or injured his captors. Harvey Cheyne bore his scars from such a battle in two raw and bleeding hands and in a back which ached more cruelly than he had ever before imagined possible!

Doubtless because of these perils of their calling, together with the knowledge that they were always at the mercy of sudden change and chance, fishermen, as a lot, were usually superstitious men. Few skippers felt safe in leaving port on a Friday just as few rarely consented to command any craft which had been launched on that risky, unpropitious day. A vessel which stuck on the ways at her launching was held to be unlucky; and many tales were current of the brief or tragic careers of those which had failed to slide easily into the water. To carry an umbrella aboard, or to drive a nail on Sunday, or to allow a hatch cover to remain bottom side up for more than an instant — all these were forerunners of ill luck and were to be avoided at all costs.

If a sea gull (and countless numbers of them in search of food were forever about, above, and even upon a fishing vessel) dropped its white excretion on a fisherman's sou'wester or oilskins, or, worst of all, upon any exposed part of his skin, the horrified recipient was so sure of some dire mishap before the voyage was over that then and there he would strip to his skin and beg his shipmates for sluicings of sea water as the only means of exorcising the impending evil or disaster!

Most New England skippers of fishing vessels strictly observed Sunday as a day of rest, re-

The ever present gulls

fusing to set their trawls on that day even when
the fish were biting well. This practice should
not, however, be set down to mere superstition,
even though it may have played its part; for
many fishermen among skippers and crews
were religious men. Not only had they been
reared in religious homes and in the churches
of their New England villages and towns, but,
like those seafarers described by the Psalmist,

they constantly saw all about them "the works of the Lord and His wonders in the deep." Whether they were of New England Protestant stock or, as in the latter half of the nineteenth century, came as well from Roman Catholic background, many if not most of them had been nurtured in religious faith.

One remembers in *Captains Courageous* how Manuel, the Portuguese sailor with the gold rings in his ears, burned his candles to the Blessed Virgin for a safe voyage and how generous he was to the priest in Gloucester, who was begging for his long list of destitute widows. One remembers, too, Long Jack, from Galway, who gave his most cherished ship model to hang above the altar of his church. Sunday on most vessels of our fishing fleets meant careful shaving and clean clothes, hours of rest and storytelling, and in many a stuffy cabin a bit of "Scripture" read by the skipper and the singing of hymns by the crew.

This religious sense is perhaps characteristic of all men and boys who have followed

The blessing of the fleet in Gloucester

through the centuries the rugged, perilous life of fishing, whatever their country or their type of faith. Tossed about far from home in small ships on stormy seas, dependent for their lives upon their courage and their wits in their hourly battle against lurking foes, they instinctively turn in discomfort, suffering, and danger to that Mysterious Power which made and rules both the earth and the seas.

I thought about these things some thirty years ago when I watched one morning from a small harbor in the Hebrides Islands off western Scotland the fishing boats leaving home for *their* fishing grounds off Iceland. Wives and children, sisters, sweethearts, and mothers were gathered on the piers in precisely the same way as in the days of sail they always gathered in a hundred New England seaport towns from eastern Maine to Narragansett Bay. As the

Our Lady of Good Voyage
carries the model
of a schooner
on her left arm

boats left the pier and began to bend their sails to catch the wind, all those on piers and decks alike began to sing in Gaelic a prayer for their safe return. The strange words rose and fell in a haunting, plaintive rhythm, sung, as I could see from the faces, with hearts as well as with voices.

A woman told me, as the sails began to fade into the distance, that this prayer had been sung for untold years and always in the ancient Gaelic, the early native language of all Celtic islands. I discovered it later in a collection of Gaelic songs translated into English.*

> *Surround us upon the fishing banks,*
>   *And quiet the stormy wave,*
> *Our Lord, King of the Seas,*
>   *St. Columba, St. Peter, the brave!*
> *The first fish which I bring up*
>   *On my hook cast into the sea*
> *The poor man shall have for his need,*
>   *In thanks for Thy care of me.*

* See Alexander Carmichael, *Carmina Gaelica* (Edinburgh, 1900). This more simple rendering of the prayer is my own.

6

Periods of Growth and of Decline

To WRITE in present times about our fishing fleets under sail is very much like writing about our clipper ships. Both are things of the past and belong to the records of our history, particularly to the history of New England. Just as our great clippers finally gave place around 1870 to the steam-driven ships of our merchant marine, so the ketches, the chebacco boats, the pinkies, and the schooners, with their sails, their dories, their trawls, and their brave men and boys have given place to the stout, heavy trawlers largely built of steel with their dragnets, their winches, their engineers, and their refrigeration plants. Fishing is, to be sure, still an industry and a vastly important one; but it is no longer the same romantic, stirring life which it was for fully three centuries, from our earliest settlements on the New England coast to that memorable day in 1905 when the first otter trawler set forth from Boston.

Perhaps there is no other industry which has known so many periods of growth or so many of decline as fishing has known, simply because it has been so radically influenced by all other changes in our country from the opening of the Great West to the various wars in which we as a people have been engaged. Let us now look at certain of these problems which fishing and fishermen have had to meet, and are still having to meet, in their long and important history.

There have been many reasons for periods of decline in fishing as a way of life. Several of these lie, of course, in the very change and expansion of our country. In our earlier centuries there were not so many competing industries. Great factories were unknown until well into the nineteenth century; there were no railroads; the vast West was unexplored and unsettled. Even codfishing itself was confined to our eastern waters and largely to those off New England and the Banks of Newfoundland.

But with the opening up of the Great West, with the discovery, for example, of the fish abounding in the Great Lakes and the salmon of the Columbia River on the Pacific Coast, the New England fisheries began to feel the pressure of competition. It was true, to be sure, that, once refrigerated cars began to be used, the fresh fish from New England could be sent thousands of miles from Boston; but it was equally true that fresh salmon from the Northwest and fresh halibut from the same Pacific region could be sent eastward to compete with the salmon of the Penobscot River in Maine and with the halibut caught on Georges Bank.

As our country grew and our frontiers advanced, the very wishes and tastes of people

had their effects on our fisheries. Our New
England forefathers were far more simple in
their desires for foods, far less demanding and
cosmopolitan than were their nineteenth-cen-
tury descendants. Meat supplied by the ever-
growing herds of cattle in our new western
states became a more popular diet, and the
former demand for fish suffered in consequence.

View of Marblehead in the early nineteenth century

Other social changes, too, have brought their
results to bear on fishing. When the beautiful
coastal regions of New England, particularly
those of Maine, began in the late nineteenth
century to be invaded by people desirous of
building summer homes, those towns formerly
supported by their fishing fleets underwent a
momentous change. Fishing piers and fishing

flakes fell into disrepair as the offshore deep-sea fishing off the Banks of Newfoundland and in the Gulf of Maine steadily gave way to inshore fishing, to men who laid their trawls and dropped their lines in nearby bays. The owners of summer estates and the occupants of summer hotels wanted fresh fish daily; and the fishermen who had formerly set forth for distant waters could now make a good and far safer living by staying at home and supplying the needs of sojourners and tourists. The shores of literally hundreds of small harbors, which once boasted their fishing fleets, bear witness in their dis-

mantled piers to this change in summer seacoast society.

The relinquishment of sail to steam and gasoline, of trawl lines and dories to the nets of otter trawlers, has in its own way added to the decline of the fishing industry even as, at the same time, it has contributed to its growth. In spite of the fact that a female codfish of average size drops in spawn some three to nine million eggs each year and, therefore, might seem exhaustless in supply of fish, no supply, however huge, can be safe against the dragging of great nets across the bottom of the sea.

View of Gloucester in the early nineteenth century

A modern dragger

Such nets, two of which are carried by the usual otter trawler today, literally clean the floor of the ocean. In a tow of less than two hours one such net can haul in some 5000 pounds of fish; and when one realizes that each boat brings back to port 75,000 to 150,000 pounds, it is not difficult to imagine that even what seems to be an inexhaustible supply will in time be depleted. For although there are laws which govern the size of the meshes of nets so that the tiny fish can escape through them, literally millions too small to be of market value are inevitably scooped up. This destruction of supply raises a most serious problem of conservation and slowly but surely must result in a new decline of our oldest New England industry.

The aim and purpose of this book have been to present a vivid picture of our fishing fleets of New England, both early and late; to give honor and tribute to the men and boys who manned their ships; to show the place which fishing has held in our history as a country; and to give a brief account of the changes which it has undergone through the centuries. Any presentation, however simple, concerning the international and diplomatic problems which fishermen have been forced to meet is not only outside its purpose, but would require a knowledge of diplomatic history which I do not possess and which my readers in all probability have not sufficient background to understand. Yet my picture would be incomplete, particularly in this chapter given to the problems which our fleet has faced, if I did not at least briefly sketch some of the difficulties and hazards which historical events, especially those of war, have brought to pass.

War has usually proved both costly and dangerous to our fishing fleets. As early as the seventeenth century during the so-called French and Indian Wars when England and France were struggling for the ownership of eastern North America and for the control of its ocean, the fisheries were inevitably involved, as each nation was jealous of its rights not only on the land, but on the sea.

Since New England fishermen did not sail so far as the Grand Banks of Newfoundland in any numbers until 1670, their part in the earlier French and Indian Wars was played largely off the coast of Maine where the French laid claim to the fisheries of that coast from Acadia in Nova Scotia to the Kennebec River. There are well-authenticated stories of Salem fishermen captured and killed by Indians, the allies of the French, and of fierce and bloody Indian attacks upon the fishing settlements at Pemaquid, Vinal Haven, Cape Porpoise, and in the region of what is now Portland. Our colonists did their part with England in her warfare to drive the French from the land and sea; and yet these early wars meant a drastic decline in fishing as an industry.

The eighteenth century also knew its wars, still between England and France, wars dangerous and disastrous to the lot of our fishing

fleets. Yet the men who manned them proved
that upon occasion they could fight as well as
fish. In the spring of 1745 some four thousand
men, at least one thousand of whom were

fishermen, captured the rival French fishing port of Louisburg on Cape Breton Island. The story of the siege and seizure of this well-fortified outpost is one not only of splendid

The Landing of the New England forces at Louisburg in 1745

achievement, but also of almost incredible daring.

Led by William Pepperell of Kittery, Maine, himself the son of a fisherman, these brave men with insufficient weapons and almost no shelter for nights of fog and rain, several of them ill from fever and exposure, took, after a siege of forty-nine days, the most important fortress in the Gulf of St. Lawrence. Perhaps the revenge which fired them after years of insult and injuries from the French was more responsible for their success than the cannon which they, like oxen, had dragged by straps over their shoulders through marshes clogged with April mud. No men, Pepperell wrote, ever behaved with greater courage, nor were any men ever more astonished by their own prowess.

It was not until 1763, at the close of the Seven Years' War with France, that England became practically the mistress of the North American fisheries; and this supremacy she was to surrender to her own colonies through their War of Independence to free themselves from her rule. One of the most potent causes of that war, as important, indeed, as the hated and more familiar Stamp Act, was the effect of the English Navigation Acts, especially of those which had to do with the importation of molasses and sugar, upon the activities of our New England fishing fleets.

Fish for generations had been exchanged in the West Indies for molasses, rum, and sugar, not only from the British islands there, but from the French islands as well. Through these new Acts which imposed heavy duties on all products except those from British possessions, New England trade in fish suffered a disastrous and hateful blow. And the Navigation Acts, in forbidding trade in fish and other New England products with European ports also, added to the consternation of our colonial merchants as well as of our fishermen. It is not difficult to see from these facts how necessary the fishing industry was to New England and how deeply it was involved in the causes of the American Revolution.

With the opening of that war the fishing vessels sailed home to their native harbors with their dories, their lines, and their bait tubs. The smaller ones remained there; but the larger ones were outfitted as privateers with former fishermen as enlisted seamen ready to redress their wrongs. War might and did put a stop to their livelihood and that of their families; but they were able and eager to fight on the seas for the rights of their country.

For nearly a decade all New England fishermen realized from bitter experience the misfortune which their way of life must face in time of war. They were to feel it again, though not for so long a time, in the War of 1812 with England when once more their wharves and their vessels were rotting and idle and when those few boats which persisted in sailing to Canadian waters were subject to seizure by British naval ships.

In our own War Between the States from

1861 to 1865 the decline in fishing was not so marked because there was little hostile activity from Confederate vessels in northern seas. What decline there was came about because of the number of young fishermen enlisted in our Northern naval forces. This was true also in the two World Wars of the present century. Boys and young men were scarce, to be sure, on fishing vessels; and yet with England and France as allies and with the necessity for food for our great armies, fishing in general prospered rather than declined.

The rights of fishing have figured largely in our diplomatic affairs, especially in the treaties which were drawn up at the close of the American Revolution and of the War of 1812. In addition to these treaties and to several lesser agreements made at various times during the nineteenth century, there have been two conventions appointed in the space of a hundred years to deal solely with the privileges and restrictions of American and Canadian fisheries, one held in London in 1818 and another in 1910 at the International Court of Arbitration at the Hague. In all these deliberations early and late many of our most famous statesmen have taken part, among them Benjamin Franklin, Thomas Jefferson,

The *Gertrude L. Thebaud* racing the Canadian schooner *Bluenose*

John Adams, John Quincy Adams, and Elihu Root.

Among the problems and questions met and discussed by representatives from England, Canada, and the United States have been the rights of American fishermen to fish in waters adjacent to Canada, to obtain bait from Canadian ports, to repair vessels or to dry and cure fish on Canadian soil, and the admission into American markets of fish and fish products offered by Canadian fishermen or merchants. Laws and regulations governing these matters have changed so many times during nearly two centuries that it would be both impossible and of little interest to attempt to summarize them here. They are mentioned only because they give evidence of the enduring importance of fishing as an industry.

Today the relations between Canadian and American fishermen are, on the whole, co-operative and amicable. Only a few relatively inconsequential tariffs are imposed on certain kinds of fish brought into our ports by our neighbors to the north; and our own fishermen are free to drag the seas off Newfoundland, Nova Scotia, and Labrador. Our government at present is slow to take any action which might result in less friendly industrial relations between the fishermen and the fishing companies of Canada and the United States.

7

Our Fishing Fleets Today

THE CHIEF fishing ports in New England today, that is, for the maintenance of fleets and for the reception and processing of cod and other groundfish, are five in number: Boston, Gloucester, and New Bedford in Massachusetts; Portland and Rockland in Maine. Each of these has its fleet of otter trawlers, the large trawler 100 feet or more in length, the medium around 60 feet; and each maintains its fishing piers to which the trawlers bring their catch, and upon or near which rise the buildings of companies given to the cleaning, the packing, and the freezing of fish. A visit to such a pier, perhaps best of all to the mammoth Boston Fish Pier,

A part of Gloucester Harbor today

built in 1913 by the Commonwealth of Massachusetts, or, as a second but almost equal choice, to one of the several piers of Gloucester, is not only a fascinating experience in itself, but demonstrates how completely mechanized an industry our fishing has become.

The otter trawlers, once they have steamed into the harbor from perhaps a week's haul of cod from the Banks of Newfoundland, tie up in a long line beside the pier and begin to

Unloading the catch

unload their hundreds of thousands of pounds of cargo. Mammoth trucks back into place ready to receive from crane-run sluiceways an incredible stream of slippery gray cod, or perhaps of haddock or ocean perch. These are dipped from the icy holds of the trawler in huge canvas buckets and dumped first into revolving wire scalers, which strip the scales from them before they are ready for the high sluiceways.

The clash and whir of machinery are everywhere. Engines of every sort sputter, throb, backfire, hum, purr. Men in oily coveralls bend above them, watching, adjusting them, turning a wheel here, moving a lever there, increasing or decreasing speed. Belts stretch and creak, slacken and tighten. The uproar is never-ending; the smells of gasoline, smoke, dirty harbor water, and fish mingle in the air.

The brown boards and bricks of the pier run with slime, blood, water, and bits of ice. The spate of fish is borne aloft up the dripping sluiceways to fall in silvery masses into the waiting trucks, which will bear them to the

Unloading part of the catch

nearby processing plants. Some fall from the laden sluices either to be gathered up by men with pitchforks and returned, or to be seized by the thousands of gulls which hover in clouds above the pier, line the roofs of the buildings like heavy white fringe, recklessly balance themselves on cranes or sluiceways in the hope of grabbing a fish, tear at those dropped on the pier, swoop over the boats themselves. Their constant squawks and cries add to the bedlam of noise. By the curb of a crammed alleyway, which runs between two lines of processing plants, a dejected old horse stands, hitched to a rickety junk wagon. He looks as out-of-place as he perhaps feels. Every now and then a scrawny cat slinks about, intent on a morsel of fish.

Though it is an impressive sight, there is little either appealing or attractive about an otter trawler. Fishing is hardly a clean business at best; yet the schooners of fifty years ago with their freshly painted sides, deckhouses and hatchways, and their neatly furled sails once they had made their harbors were immaculate in comparison with these vessels which today unload their great cargoes of fish. Otter trawlers are heavy, stout, broad-beamed boats, many of them now made of steel, though wooden ones are still seen at the piers both of Boston and of Gloucester. Their crowded decks give the impression of untidiness and confusion. On both sides lying against the bulwarks extend their long brown nets, gathered up, to be sure, and laid as flat as possible, each net flanked at either end by its huge otter board, worn and rusty from its hours in the ocean. The thick

Aboard a modern fisherman

wire cables which launch and draw the net; the heavy iron winches over which the cables wind; the high, metal-sheathed deckhouses fore and aft; the two dories carried now only in case of trouble; the decks stained and reeking with oil — all speak volubly of the revolution in our ways and methods of fishing.

Perhaps some memories of the old sailing days have dictated the names of certain of these trawlers and not without irony. One at the Bos-

Today's fishing gear

ton Fish Pier when I visited it recently bore on its stern the name *Flying Cloud*, though both name and vessel seemed a far cry from Donald McKay's beautiful clipper of 1851. Another was named *The Swallow* and a third, *The Bald Eagle*, also perhaps in irony, after another of McKay's famous ships.

The very notion of clouds in open sky or of swallows and eagles seems a collision of worlds when our modern fleets of otter trawlers chug into port and disgorge their closely packed holds. Only the water of the harbor and the countless rapacious gulls even suggest the clean, wind-swept reaches of the open sea. Machinery governs all — the clatter of a hundred engines, the quick movements of men of every race under the sun who know and control their mysteries, the departure of laden trucks for the fish-processing plants lining the streets adjacent to the pier or on the pier itself.

In all these many buildings more machinery clanks and clatters, more belts move overhead, as fish are dumped into waiting vats. Men and

women, even boys and girls in their teens stand
in rubber boots on the wet, slimy floors, some
receiving the fish for quick cleaning, others
passing them on to the deft fingers of the packers, others sealing them in tin or in cardboard
boxes, and yet others stamping the containers
with labels. A turn of the hand, the press of a
button or of a lever, and the work is done.

Within minutes the fish have moved from the
refrigerated holds of the trawlers to rest upon

a hundred piled racks at the entrance to a given plant, prepared for cooking, if they are to be cooked, for freezing, and finally, in but a matter of hours, for sail or for shipment. A week earlier they were swimming in the sea. Now, made into fillets, or balls, or sticks, or packed neck to tail, tail to neck in tin containers, they are ready to be borne away on trucks, in trains, by air, or by freighter not only across American miles of land and sea, but to all parts of the world.

orkers in a fish-processing plant

On the way to the Banks.

Such a scene as this, which is enacted on
practically any morning during the long fishing
season and in greater or less confusion depend-
ing upon the number of laden trawlers arriving
at the piers, makes it almost impossible to re-

The schooner *Columbia* converted to a diesel-powered otter trawler.

capture the life and work of the New England
fishing fleets of the past when wind and sea and
weather governed their destinies and when the
wits and courage of men made fishing our chief
industry and the basis of our foreign trade.

Today only a few aspects of that former life remain; yet these are worthy of notice.

The old *share system* is still in operation — a system which was in use on the earliest European vessels to come to our shores and which is a legacy so old that it is difficult, if not impossible, to discover its beginning or to determine its relatively few changes through the centuries. Its actual source probably lay in the highly individualistic character of fishermen themselves, in the desire to be "on their own hook," to fend and work for their own interests.

Even today on otter trawlers, as always in the past on sailing vessels, the fishermen have their share of the catch after certain deductions are made for actual costs, such as food and fuel, ice and water, and a guaranteed cash bonus for the engineer and the cook in addition to their own share in the catch. The fishermen are thus directly interested in the profits of their enterprise; and now through their labor union, which for most New England fishermen is the Atlantic Fishermen's Union, they may, like the members

A dragger's crew

of all unions, work for emendations or increases in this sharing arrangement. For vessels owned by the various fish companies which send out their trawlers from New England ports the present share is 60–40, that is 60 per cent for the crew, 40 per cent for the owner or owners of the vessel.

From visits to Boston or to Gloucester and

Tying the "cod end" knot before the net is thrown over

hours spent on their piers it is evident, too, that, by and large, the innate character of our fishermen remains. Although the dangers which faced the skipper and the crew of the *We're Here* out of Gloucester are now greatly lessened, although the sea, wind, and fog can no longer take so cruelly their toll of ships and men, life even on board an otter trawler is by no means an easy one. It still demands tremendous physical strength, long hours of labor, risk of injury and illness, absence from the comforts of home.

The fishermen who slip into Boston or Gloucester or New Bedford or the Maine har-

The Gloucester dragger *Felicia*

bors on their heavily laden, low-lying trawlers are clearly a sturdy, independent, and courageous lot in their oilskins and sou'westers whatever their native background. For, unlike the men who preceded them generations ago, they now represent all manner of races. Dark Portuguese and Italians, a Filipino or two, Negroes, blue-eyed Scandinavians, and always the Irish mingle with men of old New England stock who began our fishing as a nation.

"What sort o' trip, boys?" shouts a man on the Gloucester State Pier, waiting to catch the landing ropes of a trawler called the *Priscilla*.

The skipper, a grizzled New Englander of middle age with a firm jaw and heavy shoulders, standing in the waist of the trawler with his crew of a dozen men, answers with a laconic shrug.

"Fair enough. Eighty thousand or so, I'd say."

"Eighty thousand pounds of hell, *I'd* say!" cries a tall boy of perhaps seventeen as the trawler begins to nudge the wharfside. "My

"Lee scuppers under" in the days of sail

last trip on this dirty old tub, thanks!"

But even as he says the words, one guesses that he will ship again!

There are still farewell processions and the traditional Blessing of the Fleet in Gloucester when the trawlers set forth in the spring for the first long voyage to the Banks. Not far from the entrance to the Boston Fish Pier there is a chapel to Our Lady of Fair Voyage. Apparently our present-day fishermen, though they are far safer than their predecessors in their rocking dories, do not depend alone on modern science for their security and peace of mind.

Gloucester in 1923 erected a monument to her three centuries as a fishing port and to the memory of her hundreds of mariners lost over those three hundred years — years dedicated

THEY THAT GO
DOWN TO THE SEA
IN SHIPS
• • •
1623 — 1923

almost wholly to the fishermen's calling. It stands on a quiet street above her harbor and depicts a fisherman in his oilskins at the wheel of his vessel, daring, resolution, and strength in every line of his face and figure as he stares seaward. The pedestal on which he stands bears the words of the Psalmist:

They that go down to the sea in ships.

Index